Methuen Drama

Methuen Drama's *Modern Classics* ~~~~
from around the world. Drawing o ~~~~
launched in 1959, *Modern Classics* celebrates plays ~~~~
temporary repertoire by world-leading dramatists and presents their
work in a definitive edition, alongside new introductions by leading
scholars and industry professionals. With writers such as Pulitzer
Prize-winners Jackie Sibblies Drury, Ayad Akhtar and David Mamet
through to Lucy Prebble, Katori Hall and Caryl Churchill, *Modern
Classics* are ideal for students and anyone wanting to deepen their
knowledge of the plays that form part of the modern dramatic canon.

Beginning

It's the early hours of the morning in the aftermath of Laura's house-
warming party. Danny, 42, divorced and living with his mother, is the last
remaining guest. The flat is in a mess and so are they. One more drink?

This sharp and astute two-hander takes an intimate look in real time
at the first fragile moments of risking your heart and taking a chance.
Both comedic and tender, it asks questions about mutual loneliness
and human connections.

Beginning premiered at the National Theatre, London, in
October 2017.

'Eldridge combines a hugely sympathetic sensibility with rare dramatic power, and one leaves this exceptional play rejoicing in his
talent and impatient for his next.' *Telegraph*

'David Eldridge's gorgeous new play is a wry, funny and touching
meditation on loneliness, that private shame of the singleton in the
era of the dating app and of fraudulent boasting on social media.
Written with a real depth of insight, humour, compassion and a keen
sense of the ridiculous...' *Independent*

This new Modern Classics edition features an introduction by Sarah
Grochala.

David Eldridge's theatre credits include *Market Boy* (Olivier Theatre, National Theatre); *Holy Warriors* (Shakespeare's Globe); *Miss Julie*, *The Lady from the Sea* (Royal Exchange, Manchester); *In Basildon, Incomplete and Random Acts of Kindness*, *Under the Blue Sky* (Royal Court & West End); *Something, Someone, Somewhere* (Sixty-Six Books/Bush Theatre); *M.A.D.*, *Serving It Up* (Bush Theatre); *The Knot of the Heart* (Almeida); *Festen* (Almeida, Lyric West End & Broadway); *The Stock Da'wa*, *Falling* (Hampstead); *A Thousand Stars Explode in the Sky* (with Robert Holman and Simon Stephens, Lyric Hammersmith); *Babylone* (Belgrade Coventry); *John Gabriel Borkman*, *The Wild Duck*, *Summer Begins* (Donmar Warehouse); *A Week with Tony*, *Fighting for Breath* (Finborough); *Thanks Mum* (Red Room); *Dirty* (Theatre Royal Stratford East); and *Cabbage for Tea, Tea, Tea!* (Platform 4 Exeter).

Television credits include *Killers, Our Hidden Lives* and *The Scandalous Lady W* (BBC).

Radio credits include *Michael & Me; Stratford, Ilford, Romford and All Stations to Shenfield; Festen; The Picture Man; Like Minded People; The Secret Grief; John Gabriel Borkman; and Jenny Lomas* (BBC).

Under the Blue Sky won the Time Out Live Award 2001 for Best New Play in the West End and *Festen* the 2005 Theatregoers Choice Award for Best New Play. *The Picture Man* won the Prix Europa Best European Radio Drama 2008. *Under the Blue Sky* won the 2009 Theatregoers Choice Award for Best New Play. *The Knot of the Heart* won the 2012 Off West End Theatre Award for Best New Play.

In 2007, the University of Exeter conferred on David an Honorary Doctorate of Letters recognizing his achievement as a playwright. He is a Lecturer in Creative Writing at Birkbeck College, University of London.

Beginning

David Eldridge

With an introduction by Sarah Grochala

methuen | drama
LONDON • NEW YORK • OXFORD • NEW DELHI • SYDNEY

METHUEN DRAMA
Bloomsbury Publishing Plc
50 Bedford Square, London, WC1B 3DP, UK
1385 Broadway, New York, NY 10018, USA

BLOOMSBURY, METHUEN DRAMA and the Methuen Drama logo are trademarks of
Bloomsbury Publishing Plc
First published in Great Britain by Methuen Drama in 2017
This Modern Classics edition published in 2021

A catalogue record for this book is available from the British Library.

A catalog record for this book is available from the Library of Congress.

ISBN: PB: 978-1-3501-4617-4
ePDF: 978-1-3501-4618-1
eBook: 978-1-3501-4619-8

Series: Modern Classics

Typeset by Newgen KnowledgeWorks Pvt. Ltd., Chennai, India
Printed and bound in Great Britain

To find out more about our authors and books visit
www.bloomsbury.com and sign up for our newsletters.

Introduction

David Eldridge's *Beginning* premiered in the National Theatre's Dorfman Theatre in autumn 2017. The play tells the story of the beginning of a possible relationship between Laura, a successful career woman in her late 30s, and Danny, a divorcee in his 40s who is stuck in a dead-end recruitment job. The play is set in the small hours of the morning after the end of a house-warming party Laura has thrown in her new but soon to be renovated flat. Danny, who came to the party with a friend, Keith, finds himself left alone with Laura after it becomes clear that it is Danny, not his friend Keith, who might be 'bang in there' with her (p. 4). Despite the fact that the relationship between the couple initially seems casual or convenient, particularly from Laura's point of view, the play reveals the seeds of a deeper and more lasting relationship that could potentially develop between them.

Beginning was a huge success, garnering five-star reviews and transferring straight to the West End on finishing its run at the National. The 'brave, beautiful, intimate two-hander' was immediately singled out by critics as a classic of British theatre (Nicol 2017). It was identified as timely in its portrayal of the nature of contemporary relationships: 'the tentative (anti) romance for 21st century London life' (Mountford 2017). Eldridge's skilful portrayal of the play's two characters as 'convincingly good people' was praised. This type of character, the critic Paul Taylor notes, is hard to craft, requiring the playwright to have 'a rare gift' (Taylor 2017). *Beginning* was also identified as play that was significant in terms of Eldridge's career as a playwright. As several critics note, Eldridge is 'less well known as a writer than he deserves to be' (Shuttleworth 2017). Despite his long career and obvious skill, he is 'rather undersung'. *Beginning*, the critic Dominic Cavendish argues, is the play that should put Eldridge firmly back on the map – propel him 'back into the premiere league' (Cavendish 2017).

It should be noted that *Beginning* is not the first landmark play Eldridge has penned. He has made his mark in British theatre many times but is still often overlooked within the contemporary canon. Shuttleworth, while noting that Eldridge deserves to be better recognized, cautions that *Beginning* 'may not change that state of affairs seismically' (Shuttleworth 2017). Eldridge started writing plays whilst an undergraduate studying English literature and drama at Exeter University. He first came to prominence at the age of 22, when his play *Serving It Up* debuted at the Bush Theatre in 1996. The play is set in the East End and tells the story of unemployed skinhead Sonny and his friend Nick, whose friendship is threatened by Nick's desire to get a real job and his secret sexual relationship with Sonny's mother. While the play was identified by critics as an 'exciting' (Tinker 1996), 'brilliant' (Nathan 1996), 'remarkable' (Woddis 1996) and 'impressive' (Edwardes 1996) debut, it was also clearly identified as juvenilia. Eldridge was a 'talented new kid on the block' (Gore-Langton 1996) and though he 'was going to be a very important dramatist' (Nathan 1996), he was still in his 'apprenticeship' (Shuttleworth 1996).

Eldridge's breakthrough play was *Under the Blue Sky* (Royal Court Upstairs, 2000). The play tells the story of a relationship between a couple of middle-class teachers in their 20s through three acts in which we first meet the couple themselves in the initial act and then hear how their story progresses through casual references to them in two seemingly unrelated conversations: the first between a couple of teachers in their 30s in the second act and then the second between a couple of teachers in their 40s and 50s in the third act. The play was identified by critics as 'something special' (Taylor 2000). They praised it for both the 'intricate cohesion' (Peter 2000) of its form and the way in which it 'delicately explores male/female friendships and masculinity' (Edwardes 2000). The critic Michael Billington sees *Under the Blue Sky* as the play that moves Eldridge from being an emerging to an established playwright: 'Eldridge has been labelled "promising" ever since *Serving It Up* at the Bush four years ago. With this new play at the Royal Court's Theatre Upstairs, that promise is richly fulfilled' (Billington 2000). The critical success of *Under the Blue Sky* was followed by commercial success for Eldridge in 2004 when his 'electric, chilling and horribly funny' adaptation of Thomas Vinterberg's film *Festen* (1998) for the Almeida transferred to the West End (Bassett 2004). In 2006, he filled the National Theatre's Olivier stage with thirty-one actors playing fifty-eight roles in the 'bold, brash and fabulous' *Market Boy* (Marlowe 2006). Critical acclaim came again for Eldridge in 2011 with his 'painful and persuasive account of addiction' (Spencer 2011) in middle-class Islington in *The Knot of the Heart* (Almeida) and in 2012 with his first mainstage play at the Royal Court, *In Basildon*, a 'scrupulously observed' Chekhovian family drama set in working-class Essex (Hitchings 2012). Between these prominent productions, Eldridge's works include a number of smaller-scale productions, a historical epic and several adaptations of plays by other writers, including Ibsen and Strindberg. Despite his consistent output as a playwright, the gaps between Eldridge's more prominent productions are often interpreted as 'lulls', moments in which he recedes from the public consciousness (Cavendish 2017). Though *Beginning* is currently considered Eldridge's most accomplished play, it is a classic amongst classics, rather than a standout piece in his body of work.

Themes

The main theme of *Beginning* is the nature of love and loneliness in the age of social media and internet dating. Eldridge notes that the rise of internet dating has changed the nature of meeting someone. It has made the act of 'getting you in the same space as someone easier'. In the days before internet dating, meeting someone involved a moment of courage and vulnerability in the act of, for example, going over to a stranger at a bar and asking if they would like a drink. Internet dates in comparison are less risky, as for both participants there has already been an initial expression of mutual interest online before-hand: 'you've got the commonality of why you're there' (Eldridge 2020); 'you know where you stand' (p. 5). *Beginning* captures a moment in which two people, who live in the age of internet dating, find themselves having to deal with a potential moment of mutual attraction in the 'old-fashioned way'. They are both faced with having 'to try and find the courage to kiss and acknowledge that they like each other' without 'the crutch of social media'. Such acts of courage, Eldridge argues, are more difficult for people living in the age of internet dating as they are 'less practised' than they used to be in the kind of courage it takes to approach someone and risk rejection. The play tracks the process the characters go through to refind this moment of courage (Eldridge 2020).

Alongside this, the play examines the nature of loneliness in the social media age. It highlights the ways in which we are more connected to people as a result of social media, while at the same time exploring the problematic nature of such hyperconnectedness, particularly in terms of how it heightens rather than alleviates loneliness. Laura's feed is full of images of her friends' seemingly perfect family lives: 'making more cupcakes, or on a trampoline in their huge garden, with their kids'. The images make her want to 'scream' as they remind her of everything she does not have: 'It's like death by Facebook' (p. 25).

The play explores the ways in which finding love is different for a middle-aged couple than for a young couple. At 38 and 42, respectively, Laura and Danny are older than is traditional in love stories. Both are shown as struggling with a gap between how they envisioned their lives and how their lives have actually worked out so far: 'their dream life and the reality of their life and the disparity between the two' (Eldridge 2020). While Laura has a high-flying career, she is bereft at her lack of a family of her own. Danny has become estranged from his family through his divorce. His 'whole life's gone' and he feels suicidal about its loss (p. 64). Both characters are portrayed as 'stuck' (Eldridge 2020). Laura is throwing parties and living the same life she has been living since her 20s. She wants something more: 'No more in the gym at seven. No more foreign films on my own and a meal deal for one. No more reading every book on the Booker shortlist and making smug recommendations to Tuesday Book Club. No more just "Auntie Laura". None of it' (p. 74). Danny has regressed since his divorce and is now living at home with his mother and grandmother. Both Laura and Danny are shown as 'wanting to make progress in their lives and wondering whether progress is possible' (Eldridge 2020). The possibility of a new relationship brings with it the possibility of making progress, of finding a new 'beginning' (p. 74).

By the end of the play a relationship between Laura and Danny seems possible. They seem on track to spend Sunday together, eat a roast dinner and have 'a fucking brilliant day' (p. 61). Danny's rejection of the condom Laura offers him opens up the possibility of a future in which they have a child together. The play, however, cautions against the idea that this relationship will be successful through the image of a similar moment of possibility between Danny's friend Keith and one of Laura's employees. When Laura imagines the perfect Sunday she and Danny will have together, the audience are reminded of how this other perfect Sunday ended: 'she did a shoulder of lamb. […] He had the roast, shagged her and then drove home. And then he ignored her texts and calls' (p. 8). When Laura promises that she would never 'exclude' Danny from their child's life, the audience are reminded that Danny's wife once made him exactly the same promise (p. 62).

Danny and Laura are shown as well-matched as a couple in some elements. They both love *Strictly Come Dancing* and the same kind of food. They both want to have families. Both defy gender stereotypes in aspects of their personalities. Laura is sexually 'forward' (p. 17), while Danny likes cooking and a tidy house: 'I can't relax in here, it's like a bomb's hit it.' He is more sexually reticent: 'I don't just jump into bed with girls' (p. 31). At the same time, the couple are shown as mismatched in other fundamental ways. Laura is a Corbynite: 'I'm totally with Jeremy' (p. 22). Danny is 'a bit of a Tory boy' (p. 20). There is a significant class difference between them. Though Laura's origins are North London working class, her career has enabled her to rise in social status and become middle class. She now feels comfortably at home in the 'pesto triangle' surrounding Crouch End (p. 27). Danny is from 'Upminster Bridge' on the Eastern edge of greater London (p. 29). Though he, like Laura, went to university and became more middle class, he still feels that Laura is 'too good' for him (p. 44). In the meeting of Laura and Danny there is a meeting of the two main worlds that have dominated Eldridge's previous plays. Laura feels drawn from the middle-class worlds of *Under the Blue Sky* and *The Knot of the Heart*. Danny feels drawn from the more working-class worlds of Eldridge's East End/Essex plays, *Serving It Up*, *Market Boy* and *In Basildon*.

The play is deliberately set in the recent past. This encourages the audience to speculate, to leave them 'wondering what's happened to them [Laura and Danny] in the intervening period' (Eldridge 2020). They are left with few solid clues at the end of the play as to whether Danny and Laura go on to have a successful relationship or not. *Beginning* is not a play about a relationship that proceeds to have a middle and an end. It is a play about an inciting incident – a moment of meeting and bringing into being the possibility of a relationship that may never actually come to fruition.

Structure

The play's seemingly straightforward naturalistic structure is more complex than it initially seems. The play is set in closed time and closed space. It is a continuous scene with no scene breaks set in a single location. As such, the structure acts as a pressure cooker. There is no escape for the characters from the situation and there are no breaks in the action for the audience to relax and take a breath. Both characters are forced to confront their mutual attraction: 'the form of the play exerts maximum pressure on the characters' (Eldridge 2020). The pressure of the play's closed structure is accentuated by the fact that the play runs in 'real time' (p. 1). Most plays run in a form of condensed or accelerated time. The time characters experience onstage usually runs faster than real time. An hour of stage action often encompasses several hours or days or years of story time. *Beginning* has a running time of 100 minutes and covers 100 minutes of time in the characters' lives. In the original production, this was emphasized by a 'ticking kitchen clock' which highlights the correspondence between stage time and real time (Nicol 2017). The hands on the clock begin at 2.40 am and count out time until the play ends at 4.20 am.

The play's form is a hybrid of European hypernaturalism crossed with English domestic comedy: 'a lovechild of Kroetz and kind of English domestic comedy' (Eldridge 2020). As a playwright, Eldridge is heavily influenced by the work of the contemporary German playwright Franz Xaver Kroetz. Kroetz is renowned for his hyperrealist plays about the lives of ordinary people. For example, his 1973 play *Request Programme* tells the story of an ordinary woman who returns home, eats dinner, washes the dishes, listens to the radio and then goes to bed before getting up again to take an overdose of sleeping pills. Running in real time, the piece is completely without dialogue. The influence of Kroetz can be seen in the play's stage directions. The first moment of the play is dialogue-less. Instead, the characters hold each other's gaze for an extended period of time: '*They look at each other for a long time, for as long as you think you can get away with*' (p. 2). When Danny and Laura tidy up the mess from the party later in the play, Eldridge stresses that it happens in real time – '*It takes the time it takes*' (p. 34).

During rehearsals for the original production, the actors, Justine Mitchell (Laura) and Sam Troughton (Danny), focused on creating the world and action of the play in forensic detail. For 'every aspect of the production, there was an attempt to find a level of detail about what we were doing that made it feel very real for the two performers and the audience'. At the beginning of the original production, the audience were greeted by a set representing Laura's living room in the aftermath of the party. The placing of the party debris across the set was mapped out in painstaking detail in order to tell the story of the party that had just ended. For example, the company decided that Laura had greeted people with whisky cocktails when they arrived so there was 'the detritus from giving these cocktails to fifteen or maximum twenty people'. At another point in the evening, they decided that 'people had needed more food so she'd [Laura] ordered in pizzas' so there were discarded pizza boxes on the set. The pizza boxes were from a company called Basilico, which was one of the only two pizza delivery firms based in Crouch End that the company felt would appeal to a middle-class customer like Laura. The same level of detailed attention was paid to the portrayal of the relationship between Laura and Danny. Eldridge was keen for it to be a real rather than a stage representation of romance. During rehearsals, the company probed the difference between the two: 'what it's really like when someone says I like you? It's like "Holy fuck! What's that done to the room?"' The hypernaturalism of the play's structure has two main effects. Firstly, it encourages the audience to watch the action of the play forensically and dissect the anatomy of the interaction between Laura and Danny. It puts the characters 'under the microscope'. Secondly, it highlights the disparity between the seemingly perfect version of life people present through social media and the awkwardness and messiness of real life (Eldridge 2020).

For Eldridge, the hyper-naturalism of European playwrights like Kroetz has a seriousness that fails to fully reflect his experience of the nature of real life: 'there aren't necessarily many laughs in Kroetz'. Eldridge's own experience of dating was more comic: 'it was really important for me for the evening to have a bit of levity and for it to feel like it could make an audience really laugh as well as cry because it just felt a bit truer' (Eldridge 2020). Therefore the play mixes a hyper-naturalistic approach to representation with the tone of an English domestic comedy in the style of Alan Ayckbourn or Mike Leigh. Comic imperfection is visible from the start of the play. When the audience first encounter Danny, he is far from our idea of a traditional romantic hero. He is a mess: 'He has a big ketchup stain on his shirt' (p. 2). Eldridge argues that this blend of comedy and seriousness heightens rather than dilutes the play's naturalism. There was a moment in the original production that was created during rehearsals which perfectly illustrates the comedic nature of getting to know someone romantically in real life. When the couple finally kissed and embraced at the end of the play, Troughton (Danny) accidently put 'his hand in the fish finger sandwich' that Laura had made Danny earlier (Eldridge 2020). Despite the play's hypernaturalism, the play's structure also operates symbolically. The space in which the action takes place is a flat which is undergoing renovation. It is both 'a real room' (p. 1) and a room symbolic of the couple's hopes. It will be 'nice' one day (p. 26).

Writing process

When *Beginning* opened, critics speculated as to how closely the story of the play and the character of Danny were based on Eldridge's own personal experiences: 'Just how much of Eldridge's own life-experience has been channelled into what must rank as one of the funniest, most touching, and at times most enthralling-excruciating seduction scenes you'll ever see on stage is open to idle speculation' (Cavendish 2017). Eldridge admits that there is 'quite a bit of me in the play' as there is in all his plays. While the play feels very personal and truthful, however, the play's story and its characters are based on the playwright's encounters with a range of different people rather than his own singular experience. The play is an amalgamation of different ideas and experiences gestated over almost two decades: 'different things go into the pot' (Eldridge 2020).

Writing *Beginning* was a long and extended process. Eldridge first had the idea for the play 'nearly twenty years' ago. Its premise was born out of a 'very unromantic description' of a one-night stand that happened to one of his friends:

> There was a house party and he didn't realize the girl whose flat it was, who had hosted the party liked him. [...] And when they were going to get a taxi to leave, one of my other mates said, 'No. No, no. Stay.' At which point, you know he was a bit Del-boy-like and realized what was going on [...] after our other mates left, it was really awkward and he helped her do some tidying up from the party and then eventually they opened a bottle of wine and had a shag on the sofa. (Eldridge 2020)

Eldridge immediately recognized that this was 'a really fantastic premise for a play', but it would be years before he actually tried to write the play. The idea 'hung around': 'It was just something I fantasized about doing one day' (Eldridge 2020).

The basic idea was slowly fleshed out with other experiences. For example, the moment when Danny admits to being 'a bit poorly maintained in the area of the groin' (p. 33) was drawn from a late-night conversation with a friend of a friend in 2005:

> He got very maudlin and started to talk about the fact that he didn't have a girlfriend and that. And then he remarkably said that he was poorly maintained in the area of the groin. And like Laura does in the play, I had no idea what he was talking about. And I had all the assumptions that Laura has which is like is he telling me he can't get erection or that he's got an STI or like what is this? And then it dawned on me that he was just telling me he just hadn't had a shag for ages. (Eldridge 2020)

After this experience, Eldridge started to gather his ideas for the play more purposefully: 'I bought a box file and I wrote on the side of it "PMITAOTG", whatever the acronym is of "poorly maintained in the area of the groin"'. For a while, he gathered ideas 'on scraps of paper' or in the form of 'news clippings' and added them to the file. At this point, however, he still 'didn't really do anything with them' and after a while it 'got forgotten about' again (Eldridge 2020).

In 2012, while Eldridge was working on an adaption of the Swedish playwright August Strindberg's *Miss Julie* for the Royal Exchange in Manchester, an idea for the form of the play started to solidify. Inspired by the work of Kroetz, Eldridge initially envisioned a stripped-back hypernaturalistic version of the play: 'two people with not much dialogue'. By the time he returned to London, the play had morphed into its final hybrid form. At this point Eldridge started a series of conversations about the project with actresses and directors, which 'didn't really go anywhere'. Then in the autumn of 2015 another writing job fell through in a way that left Eldridge with time on his hands and enough money to be able to focus on writing whatever he wanted to for a while. He decided to have a go at writing *Beginning*: 'I went into my office and started on a Monday morning and three weeks later I had the first draft. It just came'. He attributes the ease of the writing process to the fact that he had been mulling the idea for the play in his head for so many years: 'I honestly think it was to do with the fact that it's the thing that I've written that I've most fantasized about and daydreamed about'. Of all of Eldridge's plays to date, he identifies *Beginning* as the 'most gestated': 'No other play has come about in that way' (Eldridge 2020).

The characters in the play are amalgams of different people. The initial template for Danny is the friend whose unromantic one-night stand sparked the premise for the play. Eldridge describes him as the kind of man 'who women really like and have always liked but he literally has no radar. He is that person where someone's trying to talk to him for half an hour and the minute she stands next to him, he walks over somewhere else'. Danny's response to his divorce is inspired in part by a friend who went through a divorce around the same time as Eldridge: 'the idea of him going on a date or talking to a woman was just like far away […] He wanted to have a beer at the weekend and go football or watch the football and spend time with his dad. He was very nervous about what next in his life in some ways'. The third person that inspired Danny was a man Eldridge met in a parenting class for divorced parents 'who'd not seen his daughters for like three years and he'd been in the courts and he was so peeled raw'. The peeled rawness Eldridge observed in this man became an important facet of his portrayal of Danny's feelings about his daughter (Eldridge 2020).

Laura is inspired by a number of different women Eldridge met while internet dating. For example, Laura's experience of 'death by Facebook' (p. 25) is based on a woman Eldridge met for whom looking at images of her Facebook friends with their children was painful: 'watching it all unfold on Facebook for her was just like death and she said the stuff about cupcakes and trampolines and all that'. Laura's forthright desire for a child is based on the unexpected number of encounters Eldridge had while dating with women who were very upfront about wanting to have children: 'there were only a handful of the women who didn't find a way of asking me on the first date if I was interested in having more children' (Eldridge 2020). Laura can be seen as surprisingly reactionary in her desires for a 'normal husband' and family life (p. 74). A few reviewers iden- tified this aspect of her character as 'cliché' (Hitchings 2018): 'she feels more representative and not quite as precisely drawn as Danny' (Hemming 2018). This element of Laura's character, however, was based on a successful career woman whom Eldridge met, who wanted to have a family before it was too late. He notes that she would 'have been fucking fuming to have been labelled reactionary' (Eldridge 2020). As the critic Paul Taylor recognizes, Eldridge is not using Laura as a symbol of what women should want: 'I don't think, though, that Eldridge is setting her up as a reactionary exemplar of a woman who recognises the hollowness of professional success only just in time.' Laura is a 'particular case', a representation of what one particular woman wants (Taylor 2017).

The critic Aleks Sierz argues that Eldridge's trademark as a writer is 'empathy, acute social observation and truthful dialogue' (Sierz 2004). *Beginning* can be seen as the pinnacle of this project. It is a play in which a writer puts a forensic lens on the moment in which the possibility of a romantic relationship comes into being and in doing so attempts to capture the real nature of romance in all its awkwardness and messiness. *Beginning* offers a warts-and-all representation of burgeoning love, which is as hilariously excruci-ating to watch as it is romantic. For Eldridge, the accuracy of the mirror he holds up to romance is his primary concern. His main aim with *Beginning* was to 'tell the truth' of a particular experi-ence: 'I think if you try and tell the truth, then that counts for some-thing. If you try and write with honesty, even if it is something that's not necessarily palatable to everyone, then you've still just told the truth' (Eldridge 2020).

Sarah Grochala

Bibliography

Bassett, Kate. 2004. 'Independent on Sunday Review: Festen'. *Theatre Record* 24 (7): 396.

Billington, Michael. 2000. 'Guardian Review: Under the Blue Sky'. *Theatre Record* 20 (19): 1216.

Cavendish, Dominic. 2017. 'Telegraph Review: Beginning'. *Theatre Record* 37 (19–20): 1077–8.

Edwardes, Jane. 1996. 'Time Out London Review: Serving It Up'. *Theatre Record* 16 (4): 222.

Edwardes, Jane. 2000. 'Time Out London Review: Under the Blue Sky'. *Theatre Record* 20 (19): 1215–16.

Eldridge, David. 1996. *Serving It Up*. London: Bush Theatre.

Eldridge, David. 2000. *Under the Blue Sky*. London: Methuen Drama.

Eldridge, David. 2004. *Festen: Based on the Dogme film and Play by Thomans Vinterberg, Morgens Rukov and Bohr Hansen*. London: Methuen Drama.

Eldridge, David. 2006. *Market Boy*. London: Methuen Drama.

Eldridge, David. 2011. *The Knot of the Heart*. London: Methuen Drama.

Eldridge, David. 2012. *In Basildon*. London: Methuen Drama.

Eldridge, David. 2020. Personal interview with David Eldridge on 12 March 2020.

Gore-Langton, Robert. 1996. 'Daily Telegraph Review: Serving It Up'. *Theatre Record* 16 (4): 220–1.

Hemming, Sarah. 2018. 'Financial Times Review: Beginning'. *Theatre Record* 38 (1): 51–2.

Hitchings, Henry. 2012. 'Evening Standard Review: In Basildon'. *Theatre Record* 32 (4): 174.

Hitchings, Henry. 2018. 'Evening Standard Review: Beginning'. *Theatre Record* 38 (1): 51.

Kroetz, Franz Xaver. 2004. *Request Programme* in *Plays One*. London: Methuen Drama.

Marlowe, Sam. 2006. 'The Times Review: Market Boy'. *Theatre Record* 26 (12): 676–7.

Mountford, Fiona. 2017. 'Evening Standard Review: Beginning'. *Theatre Record* 37 (19–20): 1076.

Nathan, David. 1996. 'Jewish Chronicle Review: Serving It Up'. *Theatre Record* 16 (4): 222.

Nicol, Patricia. 2017. 'Sunday Times Review: Beginning'. *Theatre Record* 37 (19–20): 1078.

Peter, John. 2000. 'Sunday Times Review: Under the Blue Sky'. *Theatre Record* 20 (19): 1215.

Shuttleworth, Ian. 1996. 'Financial Times Review: Serving It Up'. *Theatre Record* 16 (4): 221.

Shuttleworth, Ian. 2017. 'Financial Times Review: Beginning'. *Theatre Record* 37 (19–20): 1077.

Sierz, Aleks. 2004. 'Tribune Review: Festen'. *Theatre Record* 24 (7): 401.

Spencer, Charles. 2011. 'Daily Telegraph Review: The Knot of the Heart'. *Theatre Record* 31 (6): 299.

Strindberg, August. 2012. *Miss Julie*. Adapted by David Eldridge. London: Methuen Drama.

Taylor, Paul. 2000. 'Independent Review: Under the Blue Sky'. *Theatre Record* 20 (19): 1214–15.

Taylor, Paul. 2017. 'Independent Review: Beginning'. *Theatre Record* 37 (19–20): 1078.

Tinker, Jack. 1996. 'Daily Mail Review: Serving It Up'. *Theatre Record* 16 (4): 222.

Vinterberg, Thomas (dir.). 1998. *Festen*. Denmark: Nimbus Film.

Woddis, Carole. 1996. 'What's On Review: Serving It Up'. *Theatre Record* 16 (4): 221.

Beginning

For Caroline Winder

Beginning was first produced in the Dorfman Theatre at the National Theatre, London, on 12th October 2017. The production transferred to the Ambassadors Theatre in London's West End on 15 January 2018

Laura	**Justine Mitchell**
Danny	**Sam Troughton**

Director	Polly Findlay
Designer	Fly Davis
Lighting Designer	Jack Knowles
Sound Designer	Paul Arditti
Movement	Naomi Said

'Who knows what true loneliness is – not the conventional word, but the naked terror? To the lonely themselves it wears a mask. The most miserable outcast hugs some memory or some illusion.'

Joseph Conrad, *Under Western Eyes* (1911)

Martha   If you wasn't here with me tonight I'd go to the pictures.
Otto   What's on?
Martha   'Ben Hur'. It's an oldie, must be ten years since I saw it, but it's a film you never forget. You ever seen it?
Otto   No.

Franz Xaver Kroetz, *Through the Leaves* (1976)
trans. Anthony Vivis (2003)

The play takes place in a real room, and in real time – but stage directions are indicative, not prescriptive.

With thanks to Dominic Cooke and Robert Holman.

Late autumn, 2015.

The large living room of a flat in Crouch End, London.
It encompasses a lounge area and kitchen.

It's a bit of a mess. There's been some sort of party. It's late, the
early hours.

Standing is **Laura**, *38. This is her place. She's drinking wine.*

Looking at her, drinking a bottle of Peroni, is **Danny**, *42.*

They look at each other for a long time, for as long as you think you
can get away with.

They both jump as a door bangs downstairs.

He begins to wander a bit in the room, drinking. He evidently came
to the party after work as he's in a shirt and trousers and smart shoes.
Though his jacket and tie were dispensed some time ago.

He has a big ketchup stain on his shirt and is a bit nervous.

Silence.

Laura *sits down.* **Danny** *doesn't know what to do so he lights*
up a cigarette.

Laura   You didn't fancy it then?

Silence.

Danny   Fancy what?

Laura   Getting in the taxi?

Danny   No.

Silence.

Laura   Why's that then?

Danny   Don't know.

Laura   Don't know?

Danny   Keith told me to stay and finish my drink.

Laura   Keith told you?

Danny   Well he said 'stay and finish your drink'.

Laura   Right.

Danny   That all right?

Laura   Yes.

Laura *smiles and puts down her wine.*

Danny   Nice place.

Laura   Thanks.

Danny   To be honest I said I'd get it.

Laura   Get what?

Danny   The taxi.

Laura   What?

Silence.

Danny   Well, you know . . .

Laura   What?

Danny   I thought he was stopping the night.

Laura   Right.

Laura *laughs.*

Danny   You see the trouble with me . . .

Laura   What?

Danny   I've got no radar.

Laura   No radar?

Danny   No.

Silence.

Well it's not that I've not got one at all.

Laura   Right?

Danny   It just doesn't pick up a lot.

Silence.

Laura   Danny, what the fuck?

Silence.

Danny   You know, 'your radar'.

Laura   I don't know, Danny.

Danny   Your 'man radar' . . . And my . . . 'woman radar'.

Silence.

Laura   Oh . . .

Silence.

Danny   I curse it sometimes.

Silence.

Two people could literally be clambering . . .

Laura   Do people honestly . . .

Danny   Like clambering . . .

Laura   Do people honestly clamber?

Danny   You know, to get across the room to get to one aother. And I wouldn't notice!

Laura   No.

Silence.

Danny   No radar, see?

Laura   No. No radar.

Laura *retakes her wine and has a drink.*

Danny   I said, honest, I said 'Keith, I'll have the cab back home, you're bang in there'.

Laura   'You're bang in there?'

Danny   Yeah!

Laura   With who?

Danny   With you?

Laura   I wanted you, Danny.

Silence.

Danny   Oh.

Silence.

Like I said . . . no . . . radar.

Silence.

Laura   No, Danny.

Silence.

Danny   It's why I've taken up internet dating.

Silence.

That 'Plenty of Fish'. Dear me.

Silence.

At least you know where you stand.

Laura   Hardly, Danny.

Danny   Have you?

Laura   At least if you meet a fella at a bar. Or a party. You can look him in the eye. And make a judgement.

Silence.

Danny   Well they either like you or they don't.

Silence.

Laura   He's not my friend by the way . . .

Danny   Who?

Laura   Keith.

Danny   No?

Laura   He's just someone I know.

Danny   Right . . .

Laura   He told you we're friends, right?

Danny   Yes he did . . .

Laura   We're not. I've declined friend requests. On several occasions.

Danny   Harsh bitch.

Laura *gives him a look.*

Silence.

Danny   Like obviously you're not a harsh bitch, harsh bitch.

Laura   I should think not . . .

Danny   Like obviously you're not . . .

Laura   Well I'm relieved you don't think I'm a harsh bitch.

Silence.

Danny   I'm not sure you've got my sense of humour.

Silence.

Keith's a bit of an odd one. A cryptic one.

Laura   A bullshitter . . .

Danny   Sometimes I just say to him 'spit it out mate'.

Laura   A blagger . . .

Danny   There's no need to be so fucking spooky, is there?

Laura   Like a monumental and bare-faced liar . . .

Danny   Laura, I know he's a cunt but he's my mate . . .

Laura   Alright.

Danny   Like he's my mate.

Laura   And he's a bit of a major wally.

Danny   Babe, babe. Since when has someone being a major wally disqualified them from being your best mate?

Laura *laughs.*

Danny   Exactly.

Laura   To be fair there were quite a few major wally's here tonight. That I've not only accepted friend requests from but I've requested friendships from.

Danny   But you'll notice I'm keeping my opinions to myself . . .

Laura   You don't like my friends?

Danny   Babe . . .

Laura   Don't babe me, you don't know me.

Silence.

Danny   All I was saying is, is thinking about it, Keith has actually probably got a sort on the go . . .

Laura   What are you talking about?

Silence.

Danny   It's what I was saying.

Laura   About what?

Silence.

Does he even know where his dick is?

Danny   Who?

Laura   Are you for real?

Danny   What?

Laura   Keith . . .

Danny   Laura . . .

Laura   What?

Danny   That's who I'm talking about. I know him of old.
I know his moods and his moves.

Laura   He slept with a girl on my team . . .

Danny   I don't understand why he has to hide it. Tell your
mates, Keith. Then we all share the joy.

Silence.

With Keith you only find out about it once he's dumped
them. Or if he's got the right hump. Because they've
dumped him.

Silence.

Laura   She quite liked him.

Danny   Who?

Laura   The girl on my team.

Danny   Did she?

Laura   She got off with him at our summer party. There
was a Bollywood theme and she did look quite nice in a sari.
Anyway, he went round to see her on the Sunday and she
did a shoulder of lamb.

Danny   A shoulder of lamb?

Laura   I know. She got it from Budgens.

Silence.

Danny   Well he's never once mentioned a shoulder of lamb.

Laura   He had the roast, shagged her and then drove
home. And then he ignored her texts and calls. She ended
up sending him this long embarrassing e-mail.

Danny   Shit.

Laura   I know, I said don't click and send. But the young ones don't listen to you . . .

Danny   No.

Laura   She clicked and sent.

Danny   That won't go down well with Keith.

Laura   Why?

Danny   Well he's like a hedgehog in that situation . . .

Laura   A hedgehog? A fucking hedgehog?

Danny   Well . . .

Laura   Within a day she went from feeling a bit shit but essentially being in the right to feeling like a complete tool.

Danny   I feel for her . . .

Laura   You don't . . .

Danny   I know how that feels.

Silence.

They sound quite well suited.

Laura *laughs.*

Laura   Like she's got self-esteem issues anyway.

Danny   Oh God . . .

Laura   And like it compounded them. Massively.

Danny   If a bird told me she had self-esteem issues . . .

Laura   What?

Danny   In the blink of an eye I'd run a fucking mile.

Silence.

Laura   To be fair I read the e-mail.

Laura *laughs.*

Danny   Oh, was it cringe?

Laura   Oh, it was so cringe. And it made her sound like a lunatic. You know – and she'd been in the right.

Silence.

Danny   Oh well, he probably just changed his mind.
I would.

Laura   Do you have any idea what that does to a woman?

Danny   What?

Laura   That kind of rejection . . .

Danny   Well we've all had a fucking knock back . . .

Laura   She was going out of her mind.

Danny   Well . . .

Laura   What?

Danny   I didn't do it.

Laura   But he's your mate?

Danny   And?

Silence.

She probably overcooked the lamb. He's a bit finicky with his grub is Keith.

Danny *laughs.*

Danny   What?

Laura   You sexist, patronising, dick. You're as bad as him.

Silence.

Danny   Anyway, I'll have another Peroni . . .

Laura   If you think I'm opening your bottle for you again you can do one mate . . .

Danny   And then I'll get myself a taxi if that's alright, Laura?

Danny *drains away the lager.*

Silence.

He goes to the fridge. It's pretty sparse in the fridge. There's no Peroni but he takes a can of Stella.

He's clumsy and drops it and then without thinking picks it up and opens it. Lager froths out and spills everywhere.

Silence.

Danny   Sorry.

Laura   I'm getting rid of the carpet anyway.

Danny   I am sorry.

Silence.

Laura   Don't worry.

Danny   I am sorry, Laura.

Laura   Forget it.

Danny   I'll pay.

Laura   Don't be silly. I had the party.

Silence.

I wanted you to stay.

Danny   What d'you want me to stay for?

Laura *laughs.*

Laura   Don't be a dick.

Silence.

Danny   I often think the world would be a better place if people were more modest about their sexual prowess.

Silence.

Laura   You often think that?

Danny   And?

Laura   I often think the world would be a better place if there was peace and no war. If sexual discrimination in the workplace ended. In fact, if there was genuine gender equality and no racism or discrimination of any kind. If children were free from poverty and all kids had a good education. If migrants were welcome. If we got rid of Trident. In fact, if we got rid of all nuclear weapons. If people picked up their litter. If people stopped eating so much red meat. If people were kind and compassionate and considerate and generally nicer. All of those things would make the world a better place. But hey, that's just me.

Silence.

Danny   So . . . what like . . . made you want to buy in Crouch End?

Silence.

He drinks. **Laura** *pours more wine. She drinks.*

Silence.

Danny   You sure you want me to stay?

Laura   Yes.

Danny   You sure?

Laura *nods.*

Danny   You don't know me?

Laura   And?

Silence.

Danny   Well I have to say, I was bit, you know, shy about coming to your do.

Laura   I told Keith he could bring someone.

Danny   I'm only sorry I didn't bring a card.

Laura   Don't worry.

Danny   It's a bit shit, like coming and not . . .

Silence.

Laura   Honestly don't worry.

Danny   I did bring a bottle.

Laura   I know you did.

Danny   It's a lovely flat.

Laura   Thanks.

Danny   I bet it's not cheap.

Laura   No.

Danny   You've popped my Crouch End cherry.

Laura   A pleasure.

Silence.

Danny *drinks and starts to cough as it's gone down the wrong hole.*

Laura *whacks him on the back. Some lager comes up. He coughs loads.*

Laura   You alright?

Danny   Fucking wrong hole . . .

Laura *laughs.*

Laura   Not the first time I've heard that excuse.

Danny   I could have died.

Silence.

The penny drops and **Danny** *blushes and starts to cough again. He composes himself.*

Laura   It's only a bit of smut, Danny.

Silence.

Danny   I think the Chablis' is still in there.

Danny *goes to the fridge and looks.*

Laura   Well why don't you open it for me and come and sit next to me?

Silence.

It's a bit sad.

Danny   That yoghurt's gonna get up and walk out of there in a minute.

Laura   Get the wine and shut the door.

Danny   Is that a kiwi fruit?

Laura   Probably.

Danny   Do you need to refrigerate a kiwi fruit?

Laura   I don't know.

Danny   My mum has hers in the fruit bowl.

Laura   Does she?

Danny   She loves a bit of kiwi fruit on her porridge.

Laura   Does she?

Danny   And a banana.

Laura   If you leave that fridge door open much longer everything will go off.

Danny   There's nothing to go off!

He does as he's told.

Silence.

You want to look after yourself a bit more.

Laura   What?

Danny   Get some proper food in.

Laura   It's a waste of money on your own . . .

Danny   What?

Laura   You end up chucking it away . . .

Danny   What?

Laura   Danny, the wine.

Danny *puts down his can and gets the wine from the fridge.*

He looks around for a bottle opener. He can't find one.

Laura   I don't bother with a weekly shop.

Laura *spots one near her and throws it to him, which he catches with his free hand.*

Danny *celebrates the catch.*

Danny   Botham style.

Silence.

Laura   Was Ian Botham noted for catching the ball?

Danny   I'm not really a cricket man.

Laura   I assume you're referring to Ian Botham?

Danny   Indeed.

Danny *gets to work opening the wine. He breaks the cork as he tries to get it out.*

He struggles trying to get the other half of the cork out but can't.

Laura   Just push it in.

Danny *uses an arm of the bottle opener to push the broken cork into the wine.*

Danny *lifts up the wine bottle to inspect it.*

Danny   Sorry.

Laura   Don't worry.

Danny   I am really sorry.

Laura   Stop saying sorry.

Danny   I am such a dick.

Laura   You are.

Danny   Thanks.

Laura   No problem.

Danny   I'll get my coat.

Laura   Don't be a dick.

Danny   I know.

Laura   Come and sit down next to me and pour me a glass.

Danny *does as he's told. He pours her wine but doesn't sit too near her.*

She drinks.

Silence.

He gets up and goes to retrieve his beer. He looks at the carpet.

Danny   I think some cunt's put a fag out on your carpet.

Laura   Don't say that word.

Danny   Sorry.

Laura   I don't mind you swearing. I swear. I just don't like that word.

Danny   I'm sorry.

Silence.

Laura   Don't be sorry, just don't say it. I don't like it.

Silence.

Danny   Yeah my mum loves a kiwi fruit.

Silence.

Laura   Don't you want to kiss me?

Danny   Well . . .

Laura   Don't you want to?

Danny   Well I do . . .

Laura   Well come and be with me.

Silence.

Danny   You're quite forward.

Laura   I think you're hot. You're handsome.

Danny   Thanks.

Laura   I mean it.

Danny   Thanks.

Laura   I don't believe any of that bollocks about Keith and the taxi.

Danny   Oh no, it wasn't bollocks.

Silence.

Laura   You honestly couldn't tell I liked you tonight?

Danny   I told you. I've got no fucking radar.

Silence.

Laura   Alright.

Danny   I'm not forward like you.

Silence.

Laura   You don't know me.

Danny   No, I don't. And you don't know me.

Laura   Have you got a problem with a woman being forward?

Danny   No.

Silence.

Danny *shakes his head and starts to laugh.*

Silence.

Laura   What?

Danny   What?

Laura   You can't just laugh. And then stop laughing. And not say anything.

Danny   What?

Laura   You'll make me paranoid.

Danny   It was just something silly.

Laura   Like what?

Danny   Like I was just imagining my Facebook status tomorrow.

Laura   What?

Danny   Like 'Really hot lady told me I was hot . . .'

Laura   'Really hot lady'?

Danny   And?

Laura   Fuck's sake.

Danny   'Really hot lady told me I was hot and she wanted to sleep with me last night and I didn't shut the fuck up and I fucked it up.'

Laura   What about 'woman'?

Danny   What about it?

Laura   Woman, Danny, woman.

Silence.

You wouldn't put that on Facebook would you, though?

Danny   No!

Laura   Would you though?

Danny   No!

Laura   Over-sharer!

Danny   I was just trying to put it out there . . .

Laura   What?

Danny   The elephant in the room . . .

Laura   What?

Danny   You know?

Laura   I don't know . . .

Danny   You know, don't not say what you're thinking . . .

Laura   Danny have you got low self-esteem issues?

Danny   No.

Silence.

I wouldn't put that on Facebook.

Laura   I believe you.

Danny   I'm friends on Facebook with my mum and my nan.

Laura   You're friends on Facebook with your nan?

Danny   She loves it.

Laura   Does she though?

Danny   She loves a Facebook 'feeling'!

Laura   Does she?

Danny   Her favourite Facebook 'feeling' is 'blessed'. She's always feeling 'blessed'.

Laura   Oh my God, it's like Peter Andre on Strictly, do you watch Strictly?

Danny   Love it . . .

Laura   He's always going on about feeling blessed . . .

Danny   My mum and my nan both like Peter Andre . . .

Laura   I want to meet your nan . . .

Danny   Maybe you will . . .

Laura   What does your nan say on Facebook?

Danny   Well she mostly has rants about the Labour party and makes the odd inappropriate comment . . .

Laura   Oh my God, is your nan in the Labour party?

Danny   She is . . .

Laura   I'm in the Labour party . . .

Danny   I'm the apple of her eye and all that, but she thinks I'm a bit Tory boy . . .

Laura   She's not racist or anything like that is she?

Danny   Course she's not . . .

Laura   Oh I didn't mean she was like racist . . .

Danny   She's in the Labour party . . .

Laura   It's oldies on Facebook, you know?

Silence.

Danny   She likes *Downton* and she says things like: 'I'd ride the Earl of Grantham'.

Laura   No!

Danny   She does and she posts it on my wall!

Laura   No!

Danny   I don't even like *Downton*!

Laura   No way!

Danny   It's shit!

Laura   How old is your nan?

Danny   Ninety-two.

Laura *holds her hand up for a high five.* **Danny** *high fives her and then walks away.*

Silence.

Laura   My cousin's a bit embarrassing on Facebook. She's really right-wing. I wasn't being rude about your nan. She sounds amazing.

Silence.

Danny   She is.

Silence.

Laura   My cousin's a bit racist. Like it's bad enough but you don't want it on your time line, do you?

Silence.

Danny   My mum says it's early stages of Alzheimer's . . .

Laura   What is?

Danny   But it's not.

Laura   What?

Danny   My nan. I said to my mum 'it's not, if it was early stages of Alzheimer's she wouldn't be able to use the computer'.

Silence.

Laura   What about your dad?

Danny   Oh he left when I was seven.

Laura   Oh.

Silence.

Danny   I can't talk about him.

Laura   Why?

Danny   It's broken my heart my whole life.

His eyes fill up.

Danny   So do you like knock on doors and deliver leaflets?

Laura   Who for?

Danny   I thought you were in the Labour party?

Laura   I only joined in August . . .

Danny   Oh . . .

Laura   I haven't got any time, Danny. And anyway, I can be much more politically active on social media. I mean, I have to be careful. Because I represent my company in those spaces and on those platforms. But still. You're not a Tory are you?

Danny   Would it matter if I was?

Laura   Because I'm totally with Jeremy.

Silence.

Danny   I'm not. I'm not anything. To be honest I don't give a shit about politics. They're all liars. No one's interested in real change. I'm sorry, Laura, I just can't talk about my dad.

Silence.

Laura   You alright?

Danny   I'm not used to this.

Silence.

Laura   Man up.

Silence.

Sorry, that was mean.

Silence.

I am sorry. That was a bit harsh.

Silence.

I think things do get better, Danny. Things will get better. You know this time next year what's going to happen in America?

Danny   What?

Laura   America is going to elect a woman President for the first time in its history. And then the whole world will know things have moved forwards. For women. For everyone.

Silence.

Danny   Shall we just . . . Shall I just call a cab?

Laura   No. Don't.

Silence.

Danny   She's on Twitter an'all.

Laura   Who is?

Danny   My nan.

Laura *kills herself laughing.*

Silence.

You're winding me up now.

Danny   She is!

Laura   She's not!

Danny   She is! She does her own hashtag. Nan-tweets.

Laura   You're winding me up!

Danny   She loves it . . . She gets into spats with Owen Jones and everything.

Laura *looks at him.* **Danny** *starts to laugh.*

Danny   Got to admit, I am winding you up.

Laura *laughs.*

Silence.

Laura   I bet your profile picture is like, you at the Olympics, or you with a pie . . .

Danny   It's not.

Laura   No?

Danny   It's me and my daughter.

Silence.

Laura   Oh right. You're . . .

Danny   Yes.

Silence.

Laura   Right.

Danny   Is that a problem?

Laura   No I just didn't . . .

Danny   Think I . . .

Laura   Yes.

Silence.

What's her name?

Danny   Annabel.

Laura   That's a nice name.

Danny   Thanks. I chose it.

Silence.

Laura   How old is she?

Danny   Seven.

Danny *takes out his iPhone and shows* **Laura** *a picture of his daughter.*

Laura   She's so cute . . .

Danny   She's three there . . .

Laura   Is that a frog on her jumper?

Danny   No it's a rabbit.

Laura   Are you sure?

Danny   I bought it for her.

Laura   Sorry.

Danny   Frogs are generally green.

Silence.

Laura   Don't you see her?

Danny   No. Unfortunately not. *Silence.*

Laura   I'm sorry.

Silence.

Sometimes I hate Facebook so much. It's like death by Facebook.

Silence.

Danny   I know.

Silence.

Laura   It's like, if I see another one of my friends, or randoms from Uni, making more cupcakes, or on a trampoline in their huge garden, with their kids . . . I'll like – scream.

Silence.

Danny   Even pretend happy families look better than my life most of the time.

Silence.

Laura   Does that make me sound bitter?

Danny   No.

Laura   I sound bitter don't I?

Danny   No.

Laura   I'm not bitter.

Danny   Do I sound bitter?

Laura   No.

Silence.

Danny *considers the room.*

Danny   You're alright here.

Laura   It's nice. Or it will be when it's done.

Danny   Do you own this place then?

Laura   Yes.

Silence.

Danny   Wow.

Silence.

Laura   It's only a one-bed.

Danny   Still, nice area, Laura.

Laura   I like it.

Danny   Crouch End . . .

Laura   It's great.

Danny   Muswell Hill . . . Highgate.

Laura   I feel very lucky.

Danny   Innit though? It's the pesto triangle.

Laura *laughs.*

Silence.

Laura   Do you live in Essex as well then?

Danny   Yep.

Silence.

Laura   I don't mean to pry.

Danny   No, it's fine.

Laura   You don't share with Keith?

Danny   No, he's an animal.

Laura   He is pretty gross when he wants to be.

Danny   He sits on the khazi with the bathroom door open and covers up with a copy of *Four Four Two*.

Laura   Er, gross.

Danny   The man is forty-one years of age. It's no wonder his wife had enough of him.

Laura   I never met her.

Silence.

Danny   I don't know how Happy puts up with him.

Laura   Who's Happy?

Danny   Harry, another one of our mates. From school. He's on his own as well, though he doesn't care. That boy does not want for skirt.

Laura   For skirt?

Danny   What's wrong with that?

Laura   Like do you think you're Michael Caine or something? 'Alright geezer . . . Sound as a pound . . . Sound as a pound.'

Danny   No.

Laura   Like am I 'a nice piece of skirt'? Am I though?

Silence.

Danny   No.

Silence.

Laura   Well Harry sounds like a right charmer.

Danny   Fireman Sam, innit?

Silence.

So Keith's your client, right?

Laura   Yes he is.

Silence.

Danny   He proper made out that you're friends.

Silence.

Laura   We took Keith out for lunch. And we all got a bit trashed. And I said I was having a housewarming. And he sort of invited himself.

Danny   That's Keith alright.

Laura   He asked me if he could bring a friend.

Danny   He bothered to ask then?

Laura   I thought it was a bit of a cheek. But I thought what the fuck?

Danny   Why not?

Laura   New people. All that.

Silence.

So you're divorced?

Danny   I am.

Silence.

Laura   Recently?

Danny   Well obviously not.

Silence.

Laura   I don't know, do I?

Silence.

Danny   I've not seen Annabel since she was three.

Laura   Oh shit. Really?

Silence.

Danny   I live back at home with my mum.

Silence.

Laura   In Upminster?

Danny   Did I . . .?

Laura   No Keith . . .

Danny   Oh. It's alright. I still like it. I'm really fond of it. It's Upminster Bridge really.

Laura   I wouldn't know the difference.

Silence.

Danny   I'll get my coat then.

Laura   Don't be silly.

Danny   Yep well . . .

Laura   I really don't give a shit.

Danny   Seriously?

Laura   I like you.

Silence.

Danny   Seriously, I think I will.

Laura   You don't meet anyone when you're our age who hasn't got a story.

Danny   I feel quite . . . Er . . . Exposed.

Silence.

Laura   I've got a story.

Silence.

Obviously nothing like your story.

Danny   Thanks.

Silence.

Danny   I suppose I've got my baggage. You've got your baggage.

Laura   Thanks for that.

Laura *laughs.*

Silence.

Laura   Danny?

Danny   Yeah.

Laura   Hello?

Danny   Sorry.

Silence.

Danny   Shall we have a bit of a tidy up?

Laura *laughs.*

Danny   What?

Laura   Come and kiss me. You lemon.

Silence.

Laura   Do you like me?

Danny   I think you're great.

Laura   Do you like me?

Danny   I can't relax in here, it's like a bomb's hit it.

Laura   What?

Silence.

You've been looking at me all night.

Danny   Well, you know . . .

Laura   Come and kiss me.

Silence.

Danny   Where are the bin bags?

Silence.

Where are they, Laura?

Laura   You are such a dick.

Silence.

Danny   Let's just have a tidy up. First.

Silence.

Laura   They're under the sink.

Danny *goes to the cupboard under the sink and fishes them out.*

Danny   You don't get me.

Laura   I don't.

Danny   I don't just jump into bed with girls.

Silence.

Laura   Evidently.

Silence.

Danny   Alright?

Laura Okay.

Danny Alright?

Laura Got it. Loud and clear.

Silence.

Danny Like I'm not saying I wouldn't like to.

Laura Thanks.

Danny Like I'm not giving you the brush off.

Laura I get it.

Danny I'm not playing games.

Laura Okay.

Danny I don't play games. I like to be in the mood.
Sometimes men like to be in the mood as well.

Laura I tell you what, tidying up's really going to put me
in the mood.

Silence.

Well, shall we have a tidy up then or not?

Silence.

Danny You're pretty fit.

Laura Thanks.

Danny I mean it.

Laura Thanks.

Danny I mean I totally would. I mean I totally want to.

Laura Thank you very much kind sir.

Danny I like your hair, Jessie J. It's nice.

Silence.

Like not every bloke is like a dog with two dicks, Laura.

Laura   I get it.

Danny   Don't get me wrong. I've thought about you. In certain filthy ways in the last half an hour.

Laura   Nice.

Silence.

Danny   It's been a long time, alright?

Laura   Okay.

Danny   I like you.

Laura   Thanks.

Danny   I wouldn't normally ever say this . . .

Laura   Say what?

Silence.

Danny   To be fair I'm a bit poorly maintained in the area of the groin.

Laura   What?

Danny   What?

Laura   You're poorly maintained in the area of the groin?

Silence.

Danny   Fuck's sake.

Laura   What?

Danny   You know . . .

Laura   Danny, I don't know.

Silence.

Danny   Put two and two together . . .

Laura   I've got no idea what you're talking about . . .

Danny   I'm poorly maintained in the area of the groin . . .

Laura   What you've got a problem down there?

Danny   No!

Laura   Well what then?

Danny   I can't . . .

Silence.

Laura   What?

Danny   It's been a long time. Like a really long time.

Silence.

Laura   Since you've had sex?

Danny   Since I even kissed someone.

Silence.

Laura   Is that all?

Danny   Oh man.

Silence.

Laura   Don't be silly.

Silence.

You know, mate, you need a woman who tells you when to shut the fuck up.

Silence.

Laura *gets up and takes a bin bag from the roll in* **Danny**'*s hands.*

They begin tidying up. They tidy up the rubbish from half the room. It takes the time it takes. Glasses, crockery and cutlery get deposited by the sink. Everything else goes in the bin bag.

They're both dying in the silence. **Danny** *eventually breaks it.*

Danny   The sausage rolls were absolutely top drawer, by the way. I thought when I have housewarming for my own place. When I get one again. You know, when I'm with

someone. That's what I'll do. A buffet like that. Salami.
Artichokes. Mushroom crostini. But you still need your
sausage rolls. Your cheese and pineapple. Class that, Laura.
I had three of them. And I love a Scotch egg.

Laura   I love a Scotch egg.

Danny   Really, it's your favourite?

Laura   I have been known to smuggle a Scotch egg out of
the pub in my pocket.

Danny   I love a scotch egg.

Laura   So do I.

Danny   Good. We've got that in common.

Danny *laughs. So does* **Laura**. *They look at each other.*

Silence.

Danny   And 'I love a cheeseball.'

Laura   'I love a cheeseball.'

Danny   'I love a cheeseball.'

Laura *laughs hard, getting the reference.*

Laura   'Do you like cheeseballs?'

Danny   'I love a bag of crisps.'

Laura   'Mega.'

Danny   'Love them.'

Laura *laughs.*

Silence.

Laura   I see you had a bit of an accident earlier?

Danny   Tell me about it. Tomato ketchup's always been my
Achilles heel.

Laura   What?

Danny   When I was a kid my mum always refused to buy
me a hot dog.

*They continue tidying up until all the dirty washing-up is deposited
by the sink and on the work surface and all the rubbish has been
bagged up.*

Danny   My nan always bought me a hot dog.

Laura *gets down on her knees and begins inspecting the carpet.*

Danny   It's over there . . .

Laura   What is?

Danny   The fag burn.

Laura *heads where he's pointing.*

Laura   Fuck.

Danny   Where are the marigolds?

Laura   What?

Danny   Well I don't want to just go rifling through your
drawers, Laura.

Laura *stands up.*

Laura   Danny, it's really lovely and you're really lovely . . .

Silence.

Danny   It won't take long.

Laura   But I have to say I've got a strange ominous feeling that
I'm not going to get laid tonight.

Silence.

Danny   Don't say that.

Silence.

Laura   It's very sweet, Danny.

Silence.

You are very sweet.

Silence.

We can do the washing-up in the morning. Or I can do it when you've gone home.

Silence.

It doesn't matter.

Silence.

Can you relax now?

He nods.

Silence.

Laura *goes and sits on the sofa.* **Danny** *washes out a wine glass and pours himself some Chablis.*

Laura *lifts her glass.* **Danny** *fills it.*

Danny   Aren't you pissed?

Laura   I've drunk myself sober.

Danny *wanders over to the armchair and sits in it.*

Silence.

Laura   I'm not like this with every guy.

Silence.

Danny   Up to you what you do.

Silence.

Laura   I don't generally jump on men. I mean, you're not exactly the best candidate to be jumped on are you?

Danny   Thanks, babe.

Silence.

Like I say.

Laura   What?

Silence.

I'm not like that.

Silence.

I was with someone for ten years. I was though.

Silence.

I've been on my own for the last couple of years.

Silence.

Danny   What, you've not had a bit for a couple of years either?

Laura   No.

Danny   What no you have, or no you haven't?

Laura   I have had sex. Of course I have.

Silence.

Danny   Oh.

Laura   Is that a problem?

Danny   No. Good luck to you.

Laura   Good luck to me?

Silence.

Danny   I hope you've had loads because I've had fuck all.

Silence.

The most I can say is I've had a long tortured unrequited love affair with Aliona off *Strictly*.

Laura   You like her?

Silence.

Danny   I mean, you've got to admit she's hot.

Laura *shakes her head and really laughs. A bit too hard.*

Silence.

Danny *picks something out of his teeth and inspects it.*

Laura Danny . . . Er, gross.

Danny Fucking cork, innit.

Silence.

Danny Me and Aliona in St. Petersburg. Me and Aliona in Barbados. Me and Aliona in Disneyland with Annabel.

Silence.

Laura Jay's hot.

Danny He's so dull.

Laura He's not. He's got a bit of reserve. A bit of mystery.

Danny Dull. As. Dishwater. A grey man.

Laura You're just jealous.

Danny Damn right I am.

Laura *laughs.*

Silence.

Laura We can watch *Strictly* in bed in the morning if you want?

Silence.

We can watch it on iPlayer.

Silence.

Danny Have you had a look in your bedroom?

Laura Why?

Danny That girl with the hair fell asleep on your bed with a pint of red wine. And she had a little puke as well. And then she woke up and scarpered.

Laura *bolts out of chair and then stops herself.*

Laura   Fuck it.

Danny   Keith told me.

Laura   Great.

Danny   One of your other mates took pictures and she FB'd it. It looked quite funny actually. She already had thirty-five likes after about three minutes.

Silence.

Laura *looks at* **Danny** *and decides to go back to the sofa.*

She drinks.

Laura   Well Keith obviously thought it best to warn you in advance.

Danny   Hum.

Laura   Considerate.

Danny   Suppose so.

Silence.

Who was that girl with the hair?

Laura   I work with her.

Danny   She's a bit eccentric.

Laura   She's alright.

Danny   She thinks she's fucking Paloma Faith.

Silence.

Laura   Why don't you see your daughter?

Silence.

Laura   Why do you live with your mum?

Silence.

Laura   I got pregnant. When I was first with my ex.

Danny   Did you?

Laura   I didn't keep it. I felt like I was too young at the time.

Silence.

Laura   I've only ever told my girlfriends that.

Silence.

Danny   Darling, I am your black cab driver for the night.

Laura *laughs.*

Silence.

Danny   Did your ex know?

Laura   I wish he didn't.

Silence.

Danny   It's a nice flat this flat.

Silence.

Laura   It's my third flat. Don't you know, I was Mrs
Sensible and bought when I was twenty-three.

Silence.

Danny   Did you buy with your ex?

Laura   No, he was Australian.

Danny   You know some of those Aussies do actually like
settle down and buy property . . .

Laura   He moved in with me.

Danny   And did he earn his crust?

Laura   Why are you saying that?

Silence.

Danny   Sorry.

Laura   He worked in a bar and did a bit of general
handyman stuff.

Silence.

I had an ex-local authority place in Kentish town and then I sold that. And then I bought a flat in Archway. Although it was mine and I pretty much paid for everything I couldn't stay there after we split up. But I couldn't quite give it up. Until now. I couldn't quite give up Waterlow Park. Does that sound silly though?

Danny   The hardest thing I ever did in my life was walk out of my home.

Silence.

Laura   Will you stay tomorrow?

Danny   What?

Laura   Don't get up and go tomorrow morning.

Danny   Alright.

Silence.

Danny   You might want me to.

Laura   I won't.

Danny   Why?

Laura   I can tell.

Danny   I might be a shit fuck.

Laura   Danny.

Danny   What?

Laura   I hate Sunday on my own.

Silence.

I can't bear another Sunday on my own with a hangover.

Silence.

You want to go now, don't you?

Danny   No.

Laura   You do though, don't you?

Danny   No.

Laura   You've changed your opinion of me.

Danny   No.

Laura   I can see it all over your face though, Danny.

Danny   I haven't.

Laura   You think I'm needy now.

Silence.

Danny   I don't.

Silence.

I'll have to give my mum a bell.

Silence.

Laura   What?

Silence.

Danny   In the morning. Otherwise she'll fret. And then Mum'll be on the phone to nan. And then Nan will be posting embarrassing messages on my Facebook. And then they'll both think you're a nightmare. Before they've even met you.

Silence.

Laura   Oh you're going to introduce me to your family are you?

Silence.

Danny   I might do. If you play your cards right.

Silence.

Laura   Oh, if I play my cards right?

Silence.

Danny   Do you believe in love at first sight?

Silence.

Laura   Yes.

Silence.

Danny *gets up.*

Laura   Talk to me. Properly.

Silence.

Danny   You're too good for me.

Silence.

Laura   Even to fuck me?

Danny   I only fuck girls I might want to be with.

Laura   No one only fucks people they might want to be with.

Silence.

Danny   It's what you want, innit though?

Laura   What?

Danny   To be treated as a person.

Laura   Yes I do . . .

Danny   Not as an object.

Silence.

I've got a daughter.

Silence.

Laura   Why are you emasculating yourself?

Silence.

My life's a shell of activity.

Silence.

My parents are both dead. I've got no brothers or sisters.

Silence.

I've got money. Not a fortune, not now. But some.

Silence.

I look out in life. I look up. I look at the sky. I like to walk up to Ally Pally on a Sunday.

Silence.

If I looked in, I'd fold inside myself.

Silence.

I'm ovulating.

Silence.

Danny   You're what?

Laura   I can feel I'm ovulating. I always know. I can feel it.

The penny drops. **Danny** *understands what she's saying.*

Silence.

Laura   You don't know what it's like.

Silence.

All I'll ever be is 'Auntie Laura'.

Silence.

Danny   So I'm the spunk?

Silence.

Laura   No, I really like you.

Danny   You don't know me from Adam.

Silence.

Laura   My dad always said you can't go far wrong if you just put your hands up and tell the truth.

Silence.

Danny   Well thanks for being honest.

Silence.

I couldn't take my eyes off you all night tonight.

Laura   I know.

Silence.

Danny   It's hard to trust though, innit?

Laura   Maybe.

Danny   When you've been hurt.

Silence.

Danny   This is all taking me some guts, Laura.

Silence.

Laura   And me.

Silence.

Danny   Is it though?

Laura   I've been trying to find the courage to be with you all night.

Silence.

Danny   D'you think I'm a prick?

Laura   No.

Silence.

You returned my gaze.

Silence.

It doesn't define who I am. It just doesn't. I've done all sorts of things in my life Danny. But it is what I want now.

Silence.

Danny   Well I have to say, babe, I've spent all day on a Saturday, when I could have been over West Ham, in a room full of suits in Milton Keynes. I was looking forward to a few beers tonight. But it's turned out a bit different than I expected in the end.

Silence.

Have you ever been to Milton Keynes?

Laura   No.

Danny   Don't bother.

Silence.

Laura   What were you doing there?

Danny   Recruitment Consultancy Expo two thousand and fifteen. I can tell you, it was a hoot.

Silence.

Laura   It's like sometimes, everything you say is another obstacle. Another dare not to like you.

Danny   What, sometimes or everything I say?

Laura   Don't be like that.

Danny   I'm sorry. I . . .

Silence.

Laura   'If I say this, will she still like me now? If I do this, will she still like me?'

Silence.

I like football.

Danny   Really?

Laura   I went with my dad.

Danny   To the fucking Arsenal I bet.

Laura   To Millwall.

Danny   No! No! You didn't!

Laura *laughs.*

Danny   No! Laura! No!

Laura   Fished in.

Silence.

Danny   I wish I'd met you online.

Laura   Why?

Danny   Because everything would be so much easier.

Silence.

Laura   And how is internet dating going for you?

Danny   'How was', you mean.

Silence.

I couldn't stand my loneliness. I couldn't stand their
loneliness. They all wanted kids. Some of them were more
up front about it than others. But it was always the same.

Silence.

The loneliness. The patency of it.

Laura   Patency?

Silence.

You like to rough up your edges, don't you?

Danny   I don't know what you mean.

Laura   Play the boy.

Danny   Not really.

Laura   I bet you went to Uni and did English or something like that?

Silence.

Danny   Where did you go to Uni?

Laura   In London. In Mile End.

Silence.

Danny   What did you do?

Laura   English.

Danny   I did History.

Laura   Where?

Danny   Bristol.

Silence.

I'll never be able to afford a flat like this.

Laura   You don't know that.

Silence.

Danny   What did you give for it?

Laura   Does it matter?

Danny   Four-fifty? Five hundred grand?

Laura   Something like that.

Danny   You must have a good job though?

Laura   I'm the MD of the agency where I work.

Silence.

Danny   You're MD?

Laura   Yes. I'm the Managing Director.

Silence.

Danny   What d'you want with someone like me?

Silence.

You wouldn't look twice at me online.

Laura   I haven't met you online.

Danny   Oh, I forgot, you want my spunk.

Silence.

Awkward.

Laura   A bit.

Danny   Shall we put some music on?

Laura   Why not?

Danny   The people downstairs won't mind?

Laura   They're away.

Danny   Cool.

Laura   Hence tonight.

Danny *goes to the iPod dock and collects the iPod. He has a look through.*

Danny   I liked your play list.

Laura   D'you want anything in particular?

Danny   I'm easy.

Laura   Just stick it on shuffle.

Danny *puts the iPod back in the dock, finds the party playlist and presses shuffle.*

'Lady (Hear Me Tonight)' by Modjo plays. It's very loud so he turns it down.

The song plays on. **Danny** *speaks up over it.*

Danny   Tune.

Danny *makes a very awkward effort to dance. So does* **Laura** *on the other side of the room.*

The song plays to its end.

'I Owe You Nothing' by Bros plays.

Laura *is delighted and sings along and begins to dance as she sings. She's quite flamboyant. She encourages Danny to dance with her, but he won't.*

The song finishes.

'We No Speak Americano' by Yolanda Be Cool & DCUP plays.

They listen to the song.

Two-thirds through it she gets up and switches it off.

Silence.

Laura   So . . . You didn't feel like dancing?

Silence.

Have you got any coke?

Danny   No, don't do it. Have you?

Laura   No, don't really do it.

Silence.

I think you should just go home.

Danny   Did you plan this?

Laura   No.

Danny   You said Keith could bring a friend.

Laura   I got the idea tonight.

Silence.

Danny   And you expect me to believe that?

Laura   It's the truth.

Danny   I don't know, Laur . . .

Laura   I wanted to be near you and I just thought . . .

Danny   What?

Laura   Fuck it.

Silence.

Danny   Fuck it?

Laura   My daddy called me 'Laur'.

Silence.

Danny   Have you done this before?

Laura   No.

Silence.

Danny   And you expect me to take that on trust?

Laura   I'm thirty-eight years old and I've been sensible my whole life, Danny.

Silence.

Yep I did, I thought 'fuck it, fuck him and see what happens'. I know another woman that's done it. And. And. I like you. You've got a nice face. A kind face. You're nice, I can tell. I want my baby to have a nice daddy.

Silence.

You know, I'm quite capable of getting myself down to a Harley Street sperm bank. If I'd wanted to. Let's forget it.

Silence.

Danny   What's your favourite bit?

Laura   Of what?

Danny   The sausage meat and breadcrumbs – or the egg?

Laura   Oh.

Danny   What's your favourite bit?

Laura   Egg.

Danny   Runny or hard?

Laura   Hard.

Danny   Motorway service station dirty Ginsters or Jamie?

Laura   Dirty Ginsters every time.

Danny   Love a bit of Jamie myself. You ever made one?

Laura   No.

Danny   It's worth it.

Laura   Is it?

Danny   Nice bit of pickle on the side.

Laura   Gastropub wanker.

Danny   You love it.

Laura   All you need is HP sauce.

Silence.

Danny   D'you cook?

Laura   Oh fuck off. D'you want to know if I do the ironing as well?

Silence.

Danny   I didn't mean anything by it.

Silence.

It's hard at Mum's because the kitchen's not mine, but I try to cook.

Laura   Personally, I find Jamie Oliver a bit of a tosser.

Danny   You can't knock Jamie.

Laura   Why?

Danny   I remember watching *The Naked Chef*. I used to love it. I used to dream of having a scooter and knocking up some tucker for me mates like him.

Laura   That's sweet.

Danny   I like cooking. Genuinely, Laura. When I was married we had a massive kitchen.

Silence.

Laura   I can cook for us tomorrow.

Silence.

It's been a long time since I cooked for a man.

Silence.

I can go out for eggs and bacon and a paper.

Silence.

And I can get some stuff in for lunch and dinner.

Silence.

It's been so long since I've done that on a Sunday.

Silence.

Danny   I can cook.

Silence.

Laura   Let me.

Danny   I don't know though.

Silence.

I don't know about staying.

Silence.

Laura   Get us out of the hole, Danny.

Silence.

I only wanted to be honest.

Silence.

Danny   Nothing's even happened between us.

Laura   You think nothing's happened?

Silence.

I've put my heart in my hand and I've shown you it. Offered it. Freely.

Silence.

I've been brave.

Silence.

How brave are you, big man?

Danny   How stupid d'you think I am, you mean . . .

Silence.

You know after everything I've been through you think I'd . . .

Laura   I wouldn't know because you haven't told me.

Danny   Well you know it's only been an hour, hour-and-a-half and I'm just about getting my head around what's in your head.

Silence.

I don't know you.

Laura   How many times in your life have you connected with someone like this?

Danny   You think we've connected?

Silence.

I do think you're different. To women I meet. Generally.

Silence.

I do find you attractive. You can see I do.

Silence.

Maybe I'll fuck you later. If that's what you want. Maybe I won't.

Laura   I don't want you to fuck me. You fucking twat.

Silence.

Danny   I could kill for something to eat. Have you got a slice of toast or anything I can have?

Silence.

Laura   Are you hungry?

Danny   I'm hanked, Laur.

Silence.

Laura   D'you want a fish finger sandwich?

Danny   Do I want a fish finger sandwich?

Laura   Yeah.

Danny   That's honestly a question though?

Laura   Do you though?

Danny   Hello – earth calling Laura, mister ketchup stain is in the building.

Laura *laughs.*

Danny   I'd love one, babe.

Silence.

Laura *gets some frozen fish fingers from the freezer and then fishes some baking trays out of her oven.*

She takes one tray and arranges six fish fingers on the tray. She switches on the oven and puts the fish fingers straight in.

Danny   Fan assisted. Nice.

Silence.

Laura   I know it's a cardinal sin when you're buying to get sucked in to the fixtures and fittings as per. But I loved this oven and they said they'd leave it.

Laura *goes to the fridge and takes out some ketchup and mayonnaise.*

Silence.

Laura *notices* **Danny** *looking at her.*

Danny   I'd go a Ginsters with you.

Laura   I'd go a Ginsters with you too.

Silence.

Danny   'Crouch Endy' were they?

Laura   Journalists. Very Crouch End. Like old-school Crouch End. When I first had a look round she was on her way out with their son to 'Bongo Babies'.

Danny *laughs.*

Laura   I know. He was a sweet boy.

Danny   How old was he?

Laura   About ten months.

Danny   It's when they start to get fun.

Laura   Called Dashiell.

Danny   Oh why did they do that?

Laura   What?

Danny   You've got to pass the playground test . . .

Laura   What?

Danny   He'll get bullied.

Laura   Not round here he won't. It's a cute name.

Danny   What they staying round here then?

Laura   No.

Danny   Well then . . .

Laura   I said 'After Hammett?'

Danny   What?

Laura   They said they just liked the name. But she took great pleasure in telling me Cate Blanchett had called her son Dashiell.

Danny   Oh what a wanker. Honestly, though?

Silence.

Laura   He called him 'Dash' and she called him 'Dashy'.

Danny   I mean, that's quite sweet innit?

Laura   I mentioned *The Incredibles* but they didn't get it and they made a point of telling me 'Dashiell doesn't watch TV'.

Danny   God, they sound awful.

Laura   I thought, I bet the fucking nanny sticks a DVD on when they've gone to work.

Danny   They've got a nanny?

Laura   Yep.

Danny   God.

Laura   Even if I had that kind of money I wouldn't want a nanny for my baby.

Silence.

Danny   Annabel loved *The Incredibles*.

Silence.

Laura   I was the wanker though.

Silence.

Dashiell took a shine to me and I asked them if I could have a cuddle.

Silence.

It was completely inappropriate but I was offering asking price.

Silence.

It was so wonderful.

Silence.

Danny   You weren't a wanker. You're not a wanker.

Laura   They've bought a house in Mill Hill. I wouldn't want a nanny. I wouldn't want my kids educated privately. It's nice to have the choice. But you have to make the right choice.

Danny   We're the lucky ones.

Silence.

Laura   I've only been in here six weeks and it already feels like an admission of defeat.

I kept thinking, why buy a two-bed in an area I don't like when I can live in Crouchy . . .

Danny   At least you've got your own place. I'd send my kids to private school. I'd scrape the fees for Annabel if it meant I could see her. You do the best for your kids, don't you?

Silence.

Danny *goes to the bread bin and takes out a loaf of sliced white bread.*

He takes the butter dish and finds a knife and begins to butter four slices.

Silence.

Danny   You will meet someone.

Laura   It's not like that when you're our age . . .

Danny   You will have a baby.

Laura   Danny, that's just blind optimism.

Danny   You will. If it's what you really want.

Silence.

Laura   If that was the case I'd be married by now, with three kids and in a big house in East Finchley.

Silence.

I definitely wouldn't be making five people redundant on Monday morning. We don't call them redundancies any more. We call it 'simplification'. I don't know whether it's kind or the most ludicrous and monstrous thing I've ever heard in my life.

Silence.

Danny   You didn't know you wanted it until you realised you might never have it.

Silence.

Laura   I don't want a mirror, Danny.

Silence.

You're wrong anyway. It's something I've always wanted really. Even when I was younger.

Silence.

Danny *casually looks at some mail on top of the microwave.*

Danny   Miss Laura R Eggleston?

Laura   That's me.

Danny   What's the R for?

Laura   Rose.

Danny   Laura Rose Eggleston. You're posh, innit?

Laura   Hardly though.

Danny   Were you 'Eggy' at school?

Laura   Yeah. And 'The Ston' in sixth form.

Danny   My mates call me 'Julius'.

Laura   Julius?

Danny   No one can remember why.

Laura *laughs.*

Danny   A bloke at work – his nickname's 'Spunk Bubble'.

Laura   Why?

Danny   His mum and dad had a split condom.

Laura   Er, gross.

Danny   Don't you think it's funny though?

Laura   Fancy his parents telling him that?

Danny   And the little shit's proud of it as well.

Laura   Is he? What a dick . . .

Danny   Perhaps we should christen our one . . .

Silence.

Laura   What?

Laura *looks at* **Danny**. *They look at each other, examine each other.*

Danny *goes and sits down.*

Silence.

Danny   I would do it you know. Part of me's like – fuck it
though.

Laura   That's like how I feel.

Danny   I fancy you rotten.

Silence.

But I could do it and I could have a fucking brilliant day
with you tomorrow like.

Laura   I think we would, you know?

Danny   And we could do it again tomorrow.

Laura   I think we click, genuinely.

Danny   And then you could never want to see me again.

Silence.

And nine months down the road there'd be me and two kids of mine I never see.

Silence.

I don't think my heart could take that.

Laura   I was honest with you because I like you and I can see you're a good man.

Danny   You don't know me.

Silence.

Laura   It probably wouldn't happen anyway . . .

Danny   I'm not stupid . . .

Laura   I know you're not.

Danny   What's the chance, one in ten? One in twenty?

Silence.

Laura   You know if you did . . . And I did . . . I would never do that.

Danny   What?

Laura   You know . . .

Danny   What?

Laura   I would never exclude you.

Danny   That's what my ex-wife said.

Silence.

It's crazy we're even having the conversation. It's fucking
nuts.

Silence.

Laura   Who knows what's going to happen?

Danny   I fucking wish you'd kept your mouth shut and said
nothing and just fucked me.

Laura   No Danny . . .

Danny   And held me and told me nothing and given me an
amazing night tonight and day tomorrow.

Laura   Danny . . .

Danny   I need someone to hold me as well. You think a
man doesn't need that?

Laura   I never said that . . .

Danny   You think a man doesn't need warmth and love?

Laura   I know, I need it . . .

Danny   Why couldn't you just give me that and give
yourself that?

Laura   I wanted to . . .

Danny   And deal with your guilt . . .

Laura   Danny, I can't use someone like that.

Silence.

Danny   You think you're the only one that's lonely?

Silence.

I thought nothing could be lonelier than an unhappy
marriage. But I tell you it's got nothing on sitting there with
your mum and your nan on a Monday night after work. And
you've got absolutely nothing to say to each other though.
Nothing. And you're forty-two years of age. And all you can
think of is your daughter you've not seen for four years. And

what happened at school that day. And whether she's going
to dancing classes or learning to play the violin. And you go
up to your room. The room that was your room when you
were a kid. And it's still got the claret and blue on the walls.
And you see the toy box in the corner. That was your toy box
when you was a kid. Except now it's full of your daughter's
toys from. Four years ago though. Peppa Pig and, and . . .

Silence.

And you haven't got a clue what she's into now. Or whether
she even remembers you. And knows she's got a dad. Your
own flesh and blood.

Silence.

Your whole life's gone. Everything you were certain of. It's
gone.

Silence.

I'd top myself if I knew it wouldn't devastate my mum and
my nan. I'd do it though.

Silence.

I'm not even a shell, babe. I'm candy-floss an hour out of the
maker.

Silence.

When the train was coming in to take us back to Euston this
afternoon. I went there. In my head.

Silence.

And I looked at those idiots that I work with. And I thought,
I won't give you a fucking story that'll be an office joke
within a week.

Laura   Fucking hell, Danny. If you're gonna do it, don't do it in
Milton Keynes.

Danny *starts to laugh. He wants to cry but he doesn't let himself cry
in front of* **Laura**.

Silence.

Danny   You make me laugh.

Silence.

Laura   You'd never do anything like that.

Danny   No, I wouldn't.

Laura   I can tell.

Danny   I worry I'll never see Annabel again.

Silence.

Laura   It must be lonely.

Danny   It is.

Laura   It must be a lonely thing to live with?

Danny   You frighten me. They way you look at me. You unpeel me.

Silence.

It makes me think about the man I was.

Silence.

I'm the bloke in the park on a Sunday morning. Having a fag. Watching every other dad with their kids. What's wrong with you, Laura? You can't just decide things like this on a whim . . .

Laura *screams.*

Laura   You think I want a baby on a whim!

Silence.

Danny   I'm sorry.

Silence.

Laura   Don't worry.

Danny   I'm sorry, Laura.

Laura *goes to the oven and takes out the fish fingers.*

She makes two fish finger sandwiches and puts lots of ketchup and mayonnaise on both of them.

She gives **Danny** *his sandwich and then returns and collects hers.*

She eats hers. He doesn't touch his. She finishes her sandwich.

Laura   Why don't you see Annabel?

Danny   Because she lives in Truro now.

Laura   Then get a lawyer.

Danny   I've got no money left. She's gone back to Cornwall.

Silence.

Her mother does what she likes. She's so much like me.
Annabel. She's the spit of me.

Silence.

I'm a monthly direct debit. That's all I am.

Silence.

Danny   *lights up a cigarette and smokes.*

Silence.

Laura   We moved here when I was thirteen. When Mum
met Dad. And we lived on Landseer Road. I was there until
I went to Uni. It was just me and Mum and Dad. He was
always my dad. I took his name when Mum did. My dad was
a postman and my mum was a teacher. We were a unit.

Silence.

My mum got ovarian cancer when I was twenty and she was
dead six months later.

Silence.

It was awful. But in a way it was a lot worse seeing what happened to Dad, though. He was always a modest drinker. Half of ale, half of bitter. But when Mum went Dad drank.

Silence.

He drank a lot. He smoked. He smoked all the time when she was gone. I think he found it hard to be around me. He said I'm so much like Mum. He was dead within three years.

Silence.

I was amazed he managed to hold down his job until he died.

Silence.

He left me some money. There wasn't much. He'd not been paying the mortgage. He was a law unto himself once mum had gone. You couldn't tell him anything. Is that you?

Silence.

Danny   No, Laur.

Silence.

Laura   I don't need a man. I don't need you. Not really.

Silence.

I'm not desperate for a man. I'm quite happy on my own.

Silence.

Eat your sandwich, Danny.

Danny *does as he's told and eats his sandwich. He stops and looks at her.*

Danny   How would it work then?

Laura   What?

Danny   If we go to bed.

Laura   Er, I don't know about my bed.

Danny   The sofa then.

Silence.

Laura   We'd just do it.

Danny   And?

Laura   And we'd cuddle up and go to sleep.

Danny   And what then?

Laura   And then we'd do it again in the morning.

Danny   And what after that?

Laura   I'd go out to get breakfast, like I said I would.

Danny   And you'd see me again?

Silence.

Laura   I don't know. I think I would. I honestly don't know. I can't say any more than I've said to persuade you. It's not right. I don't know, Danny.

Silence.

Danny   All I've ever wanted is to be is a family man.

Laura   I can see that.

Silence.

Danny   Do you promise me if I do what you want and if it happens and you know . . . You . . . You'll always include me?

Silence.

Laura   They'd always know their dad.

Silence.

Danny   Do you promise me you'd always include me?

Laura   I can't make that promise, Danny. I don't know you.

Silence.

You don't have to do anything you don't want to do. I've been completely up front with you.

Silence.

Danny   But Annabel?

Laura   What about her?

Danny   She'd have a brother or a sister . . .

Laura   I can't help you with your ex.

Silence.

Danny   So it's your call? It's going to be your call . . .

Laura   Yeah, I think it is.

Silence.

Danny   So it's a punt?

Silence.

Laura   Or maybe the beginning of something.

Silence.

Laura   Why did you split up with your wife?

Danny   We stopped listening to each other.

Silence.

Laura   And that ended a marriage?

Silence.

Danny   We stopped talking to each other.

Laura   That's sad.

Danny   We had Annabel. A home. But we didn't have each other. We had Annabel but we forgot everything else we had in common.

Silence.

Laura   That is sad.

Danny   Yep.

Laura   Especially for Annabel.

Silence.

Danny   I had an affair.

Silence.

Laura   I did wonder.

Silence.

Danny   It was . . .

Laura   What?

Danny   I don't know.

Silence.

Laura   D'you have regrets?

Silence.

Danny   I don't know if I can talk to you about this yet.

Silence.

Laura   That's fine.

Danny   You get it though, right?

Laura   Of course I do.

Silence.

Are you still in love with her?

Danny   Who?

Silence.

My wife?

Laura   Well, I guess . . .

Danny   No . . .

Laura   I meant . . .

Danny   Her?

Laura   I guess so – yes. The woman who . . .

Danny   No, no, I'm not.

Silence.

Laura   I mean, it's none of my business.

Danny   It's fine.

Laura   It isn't though.

Danny   I don't mind you asking . . .

Laura   Really . . .

Danny   As long as you don't mind if I don't want to talk about it.

Silence.

Laura   Of course I don't.

Danny   I feel ashamed.

Laura   Oh don't . . .

Danny   I feel I let myself down . . .

Laura   No . . .

Danny   And I feel like I let Annabel down.

Laura   Don't though.

Danny   It's true. I'm not a bad man.

Silence.

Laura   If you knew everything about my life you wouldn't like me.

Silence.

Danny   I don't think there's a person in this world you could say any different about.

Silence.

I don't care what your past is.

Silence.

I care about now. The now. It's all I care about, Laura. How d'you want to live your life now? What d'you want to do now?

Laura   You know.

Silence.

Danny   Tell me what you want.

Laura   You know what I want.

Danny   Tell me about what happens next.

Silence.

Laura   You walk towards me and kiss me.

Danny   I kiss you.

Laura   We kiss like it's the kiss that makes you feel like you're home.

Silence.

You take my hand and we sit next to each other. With ease, though.

Danny   With ease?

Laura   And we kiss again. You undress me.

Silence.

Everything apart from my knickers. And you kiss me as you undress me. My eyelids, my neck, my shoulders, my breasts, my tummy. But you don't touch me. Not yet. You kiss my thighs, my calves, my heel, my little toe. And then you rise.

Silence.

And I undress you. Slowly. Carefully. Kissing. Just kissing.
You let me touch you.

Silence.

Danny   It's been a while . . .

Laura   I know . . .

Danny   I think you might be better off letting me get in
there.

Laura *laughs.*

Danny *lights a cigarette. He thinks. He puts it out.*

Silence.

Laura   We fall asleep on the sofa for a bit. We get up and
turn the mattress over on my bed and change the bedding
and we sleep. You know about tomorrow. But tomorrow
night. Sunday night. When it's time for you to go. You say
you're staying. You ring your mum. And she rings your nan.

Danny *laughs.*

And you tell her that you're not coming home.

Silence.

We get the W7 to Finsbury Park and kiss each other goodbye
at King's Cross, when you get off. But you go and buy a
clean shirt and some deodorant though. And then you go to
work. And I go to work. And as I walk up Tottenham Court
Road I think about you. And I dream.

Silence.

I dream like I haven't dreamt in years.

Silence.

Of coming home and you coming home to me, and me to
you. And I'll know in my heart I'll never be lonely again.

Silence.

No more giving everything to work. Because already life is beginning.

Silence.

In a year this place is sold and there's me and you and . . .

Laura *wants to cry. She won't cry in front of him.*

Silence.

No more in the gym at seven. No more foreign films on my own and a meal deal for one. No more reading every book on the Booker shortlist and making smug recommendations to Tuesday Book Club. No more just 'Auntie Laura'. None of it.

Silence.

What's wrong with that?

Silence.

What's wrong with wanting to have a family and be married and be normal though?

Silence.

My friends are all so jealous of my independence. My career. My courage embracing being on my own. My travelling. My dates, my lovers, my embarrassing nights out.

Laura *screams.*

But it's so, so, so . . . You know?

Danny *nods.*

Silence.

Laura   I want a people carrier. I want a big house in Essex. I want kids. I want a family. I want a husband. I want to work from nine till five Monday to Thursday and then have the day on a Friday to be with my son or my daughter. I want to be married. And I want a normal husband I can rely on. And I still want a fucking white dress. And I want to put all the pictures on Facebook. Every last single one, though. I want pictures of you kissing me on the steps of the church. Of you dancing with me to Bros. Of you carrying me up to our room when I'm totalled at the end of the night. I want pictures of me with your mum and your nan. Who both love me. I want pictures of us with our baby. I want pictures of me making cupcakes with him. Or her. Or him. Or her. I want the place on the Amalfi coast. I want to be a size fourteen. I want us to go to the opera and you to wear black tie. Just because we've never done anything like it before and maybe we'll never do it again because we hate it. But we'll laugh. We'll laugh ourselves sick with laughing. We'll turn fifty and start looking the same. Me with short hair. And us in matching body warmers. And we'll cruise. We'll go on a cruise just like my mum and dad did. Before they died.

Silence.

But we won't die young like them. We'll be like the couple I saw at Heathrow.

Silence.

Eighty, maybe ninety. Him in a jacket and trousers. And her in a long elegant violet dress. Holding hands. Holding hands and never letting go.

Silence.

Danny   I'll never be able to give you that.

Laura   I know.

Silence.

Danny   I've got nothing.

Silence.

Laura   I know.

Silence.

Danny   You need a man who can give you the life you want.

Laura   I don't want a cunt with an Audi.

Silence.

I want The You. I want The You. That's what I want.

Silence.

Danny *goes to her and kisses her. They kiss.*

Danny *takes her hand and leads her to the sofa.*

They kiss again.

Danny *begins to undress her. Slowly, kissing as he goes. Until she's just in her bra and knickers.*

Laura *kisses him and removes his shirt. She kisses as she goes.*

Laura *undoes his belt.* **Danny** *stands and his trousers fall.*

Danny *moves away slightly and takes off his socks.* **Laura** *stands.*

They both look at each other in their underwear.

Silence.

Danny   I'm sorry about my . . .

Laura   What?

Danny   My belly.

Silence.

Laura   You'd do this?

Danny   I don't want to talk any more.

Silence.

Laura   I'm scared now.

Danny   Don't be scared.

Laura   I am.

Danny   Don't be.

Laura   I feel like my whole life's on the toss of a coin.

Silence.

Laura *thinks, makes a decision and goes to find her handbag. It takes a while, but she finds it.*

She roots around inside and takes out her purse. She fishes out a condom.

She offers it to **Danny**.

Danny   Right.

Laura   I want to though.

Danny   Laur . . .

Laura   Laura.

Danny   I'm cool with it.

Laura   If you still like me. And I still like you. In the morning then we can . . .

Danny   I am cool with it . . .

Laura   I've only got this one anyway.

Silence.

Something changed when you came tonight. And you looked at me.

Silence.

Danny   Same.

Laura   I know.

Silence.

I've got to trust that though.

Danny   I get it, babe.

Silence.

Is there any chance you can flick the heating on?

Laura   What?

Danny   I feel like the last chicken in Sainsbury's.

Laura *really laughs.*

Silence.

Laura *goes to* **Danny** *and holds him. They just hold each other.*

Laura   You getting warmer?

Danny   Not yet.

Laura   Just give it a minute.

Silence.

Danny   If you tell me where the thermostat is though . . .

Laura *lets him go, goes to the dial on the wall and turns up the heating.*

She stays where she is and looks at him.

Laura   You don't think this is crazy?

Danny   No.

Laura   You sure?

Danny   When has anyone ever got it on with anyone and it's not felt crazy?

Silence.

Like even a tiny bit.

Silence.

Laura   I think you're amazing doing this.

Danny   Why?

Laura   When I put my cards on the table I was expecting you to just walk out.

Danny   Why would I automatically do that?

Laura   I don't know, I . . .

Silence.

Danny   Laura, you're the brave one.

Laura   I'm trying to be.

Laura *smiles.*

You're absolutely sure?

Danny   Yeah.

Laura   We're good people. You and me. Come here.

Silence.

I want a good beginning.

Danny *nods.* **Laura** *advances towards* **Danny** *and they kiss.* **Danny** *takes her hand and leads her towards the sofa.*

He takes the condom from her and looks at it. He thinks, makes a decision and places the condom gently to one side. They kiss.

Fade. The End.